Original title:
Warm Hearts, Frosty Nights

Author: Helena Marchant
ISBN HARDBACK: 978-9916-90-956-0
ISBN PAPERBACK: 978-9916-90-957-7

Fireside Whispers

The fire crackles, pops with glee,
It stole my marshmallows, oh me, oh my!
S'mores are now a distant dream,
I might just roast my socks, oh why!

The logs are dancing, flames they tease,
A shadow puppet show, if you please!
I'm stuck in this chair, can’t seem to stand,
I shout for help, but it's just the band.

Stars Against the Cold

The cold creeps in, but stars are bright,
I thought I'd bring my dog for a night.
He twirls around, a furry comet,
But all he wants is to chew my bonnet!

The constellations wink and chuckle,
As my hot cocoa starts to bubble.
One sip too much, and I spill with glee,
Now it's a puddle, not just for me.

Huddled Together Under Stars

Huddled close, we share a snack,
But someone stole the last Nutri-Grain pack.
It’s a mystery who’s the hungry thief,
We all blame the dog in disbelief.

The stars above are bright and bold,
Yet here I am, wrapped in my scarf so old.
A comet zooms by, oh what a sight,
But I’m busy fighting off a sneeze—what a fright!

The Glow of Cozy Moments

The glow of warmth, with socks so thick,
I swear these toes could make a kick.
I thought that I would find romance,
But all I got was a clumsy dance.

With laughter echoing in the room,
I tripped over the rug, oh what gloom!
The cozy moments turn to a show,
And now my coffee's spilled all aglow.

Heartfelt in the Glacial Silence

In glaciers deep, my heart does freeze,
But penguins waddle with such great ease.
I shout my love, it echoes so shy,
The icebergs giggle as they pass by.

A snowman's smile is warm and wide,
He's my companion on this chilly ride.
With frosty breath, I declare my fate,
Love blooms in places where it's cold and late.

Songs by the Firelight

By the fire, I sing of my socks so bright,
They've got holes, but they're quite a sight.
The flames dance wildly, swaying like me,
As marshmallows roast with sad glee.

A squirrel nearby joins in the tune,
He's stealing my nuts; I'm howling at noon.
With laughter echoing throughout the night,
I'll serenade shadows with all my might.

Wrapped in Muffled Joy

Wrapped up snug in my blanket's fold,
I share my snacks; they're worth more than gold.
I hear my neighbor's dog, he howls a tune,
While dreaming of chasing the world's biggest moon.

My cat's in a ball, he looks like a fur,
A purring machine—that's my kind of blur.
Wrapped up in joy, we twirl and play,
Awake in a dream, we'll waste the day.

The Touch of Heat

The sun beats down, and I start to melt,
Like ice cream cones with poor self-help.
I shuffle along on feet of goo,
In search of shade that's slightly askew.

A popsicle slips, oh what a sight!
My face looks sad but my heart's feeling light.
Lemonade stands are the epic quest,
For the touch of heat makes my thirst manifest.

Softly Falling Icicles

Icicles hang like daggers,
Stabbing at my forehead.
I duck and weave with laughter,
Who knew ice could cause dread?

They plunge down with a splatter,
On the unsuspecting ground.
A winter's game of dodgeball,
With no referee around.

Each one a frozen random,
Of water's playful tease.
As they crash, I wonder,
Will they freeze my shivering knees?

Yet in this icy chaos,
I can't help but just grin.
Let them fall and clatter,
I'll just stay safe within.

A Symphony of Sips

Tea steeping in the kettle,
A symphony, I cheer.
With every slurp and gulp now,
It's music to my ear.

Coffee brews a bold note,
A caffeinated shout.
While milk shakes up the rhythm,
Silly moos, no doubt.

Hot cocoa's sweet addition,
With marshmallows that dance.
My mug becomes a stage,
For the sugar-coated prance.

So raise your cups in chorus,
And add a dash of cheer.
For every sip a giggle,
Brings our worries near.

Laughter in the Frigid Air

Cold air nips with mischief,
Each breath a frosty puff.
I laugh and stretch my arms wide,
Winter's playful stuff.

Snowflakes tumble, twist and swirl,
Like dancers in the night.
I leap and dodge as they fall,
This is pure delight!

Ice on my nose like jewels,
The chilly air does sting.
But every laugh that echoes,
Feels like a warm spring fling.

So here’s to frosty giggles,
And winters cold embrace.
In laughter's bright reflection,
We find our happy place.

Glowing Spirits

The moonlight's soft caress,
On snowflakes here they play.
I lift my glass and cheer,
To spirits on display.

A winter pub with friends,
We gather round the fire.
With tales of yesteryears,
And dreams that never tire.

Each toast a glowing moment,
With laughter interwoven.
Hot cider in our hands,
Our hearts are gently golden.

So raise the cup for merriment,
And let the good times roll.
In this warm winter cabin,
We're kindred spirits, whole.

Heat in a Frozen Realm

In a kingdom of ice, where penguins parade,
I tried to make tea, but my kettle just stayed.
It danced on the stove, ice cream in the pot,
I guess boiling water is what I forgot.

Snowflakes like popcorn drift down from the sky,
I wore my warm mittens, oh my, oh my!
But my nose is still frozen, my toes have gone numb,
I'm starting to think that I'm turning to gum.

Frost-kissed Moments

The snowflakes are laughing, they tickle my cheeks,
While icicles dangle like overgrown beaks.
I tried to build a snowman, but he lost his head,
Now he's just a pile, a frosty old spread.

The winter sun shines, but it brings only mist,
My hot cocoa's frozen, I’m clenching my fist.
Ice is my enemy, it never behaves,
I slipped on the driveway and danced like a wave.

A Lantern's Gentle Glow

A lantern hangs low, with a flicker and sway,
It whispers to shadows that dance and that play.
With bugs in a panic, they fly all around,
Who knew light could lead to such chaos profound?

The glow draws in critters, they gather like trolls,
My guests from the garden, all jostling for roles.
But with one little breeze, they scatter and dart,
Leaving me with a lantern and an empty heart.

Cozy Lamentations

Wrapped up in a blanket, I ponder my fate,
The fridge is my friend, but it's getting too late.
My snacks are all gone, it's a sad little sight,
I thought I had chips, but they vanished in the night.

The couch hugs me close, but my dreams start to fade,
I find comfort in crumbs, but I'm feeling betrayed.
With drowsy lamentations, I start to conspire,
Perhaps a midnight feast? That's one way to retire!

Wrapped in Love

In a quilt of hugs we lay,
With snacks for each, come what may.
The dog dreams loud, what a sight,
While we both giggle at the night.

Each wrinkle tells a story bright,
Of pizza nights and pillow fights.
Your snore's a tune, I know it well,
It’s music to my heart’s own swell.

When popcorn pops, it flies around,
Like confetti in our cozy mound.
Wrapped in love, we count sheep's flight,
Adventure in dreams till morning light.

Chasing Away the Chill

The winter winds are howling loud,
But we're inside, all snug and proud.
With cocoa hot and smiles so wide,
We'll chase away the chill outside.

The thermostat's our best friend here,
As we layer up with lots of cheer.
Your fuzzy socks are quite a find,
They make my feet feel quite aligned.

We dance around to silly tunes,
In sweatshirts fit for big raccoons.
The chill may tingle at our toes,
But laughter's warmth is what we chose.

The Warmth We Share

A couch so soft, a perfect nest,
Your silly jokes are simply the best.
With popcorn, pillows, and love to spare,
Together, we make the perfect pair.

We gather all our favorite things,
Like puns and dreams and silly swings.
In every giggle, in every sigh,
Our warmth ignites like fireflies.

The heater hums, a soothing sound,
While outside it’s snowy and round.
With flickering lights and hearts ablaze,
In our little bubble, we'll always stay.

A Blanket of Starlight

The stars above shine like your smile,
They twinkle down to make us stay awhile.
Under this blanket, so cozy and bright,
We chase our worries into the night.

With laughter echoing throughout the space,
We play hide and seek with moon's warm embrace.
The universe knows our fun-loving quest,
As we share our dreams, we feel so blessed.

In this blanket of starlight we dwell,
Where every story is ours to tell.
With wishes whispered to the sky above,
Under these stars, we're wrapped in love.

Comfort Found in the Silence of Snow

Winter blankets the ground, so white,
A snowman stares, a comical sight.
My dog leaps in joy, a snowball chase,
While I trip on ice, in an awkward race.

Snowflakes dance like they're on a spree,
Turning my garden into a snowy sea.
Each crunch underfoot, a tiny delight,
Except when it's my bottom that takes flight!

Serene Heartbeats Amidst the White

The world slows down, the air feels light,
Snowflakes land softly, a pure white sight.
I sip hot cocoa, trying to relax,
While the cat plots a pounce, planning attacks.

Footprints appear, then vanish with glee,
Like secrets whispered by the old oak tree.
Oh, what a scene! So calm and true,
Until I slip and shout—'Watch out, you too!'

Hugging Memories Under a Frosty Veil

Nostalgia wraps like a scarf snug and tight,
Carols bring laughter on this chilly night.
Each holiday movie, a rerun delight,
Especially that one where cats start to fight.

Letters to Santa, I’m still on the list,
Though some gifts were things that nobody wished.
I dream of warm cookies, fresh from the oven,
Instead, the cat snacks on crumbs; how he's lovin’!

Shared Secrets by Candlelit Nights

Candles flicker as shadows dance,
Stories unfold, like a second chance.
We giggle at memories we wish to keep,
And laugh at the time I fell asleep!

Whispers of secrets, we treasure like gold,
Trying to decode what the cat has told.
The fire crackles, throwing sparks in the air,
While we draft plans, perhaps a dare to share!

Comfort in the Silence

In a world so loud, I find some peace,
A quiet spot where worries cease.
The dog snores softly, the cat's a lump,
With snacks nearby, I'm the king of the dump.

The clock ticks slow, it's a lazy affair,
I sip my tea, without a care.
Thoughts drift like clouds, oh so airy,
Who needs a party? This is quite merry!

The silence speaks in whispers clear,
What’s more cozy than this right here?
With each steamy sip, I contemplate,
Should I eat dessert? Yes, that’s first-rate!

So here's to moments, wrapped in still,
Where silence wraps us, like a warm chill.
In comfort found, I hold it tight,
Easy does it, till the morning light.

Love Underneath a Frosted Sky

Underneath the frosty glow,
We share a laugh, two hearts in tow.
With noses red and hands held tight,
We dance around like kids in flight.

Snowflakes tumble, landing here,
A chilly kiss brings us near.
With hats askew and mittens lost,
Love in winter is worth the cost.

The hot cocoa spills, oh what a sight,
We giggle and shiver, oh what delight!
With every sip, warmth is gained,
Who knew love could be so unchained?

So here we stand, frosted and bright,
Underneath this sky, pure as white.
Let winter winds blow, we won't budge,
For love and laughter, we'll always trudge!

Breaths Like Frost

Breaths like frost on a chilly morn,
Soft whispers dance, as new days are born.
With every puff, a cloud I make,
Warning to pets, "Don't give me a shake!"

Little puffs, they float and sway,
Catching sunlight, then drifting away.
I chase them down, like kids in play,
Oh, the things we do in a frosty ballet!

"Do you see that one?" I say with glee,
"A dragon! A castle! Could that be me?"
But all that's left is a breath of air,
Turns out, I'm talking to nowhere, I swear!

So here I breathe, and pretend to see,
Worlds made of frost, just my cup of tea.
Crafting dreams with every puff,
Winter's magic can't be too tough!

Tales told by Firelight

Gather ‘round, the fire's bright,
Tell me tales of fanciful night.
With shadows dancing on the wall,
I swear it’s Bigfoot, not just my pal!

Once upon a time, with snacks in sight,
We fancied ourselves as brave knights.
But our quest quickly turned to quests for chips,
With treasure maps made of salty dips!

A wandering ghost, or maybe just me,
Snoozing away, sipping sweet tea.
We tell tall tales until we yawn,
What happened next? The plot’s all gone!

So here we sit, with tales so bold,
Sharing laughter, as night grows cold.
With firelight glowing, we hold so tight,
To every whimsy, lost in the night.

Nostalgic Tales by the Fire

In the glow of flames, we sit,
Recalling how we fell in the bit.
A tale of socks that went awry,
And how the cat learned to fly.

Grandpa's stories, oh so bold,
About the days of yore retold.
When phones were bricks, and pens would leak,
And every word took hours to speak.

We laugh at fashion: stripes and checks,
And wonder how we looked with specs.
With marshmallows charred, we toast a ghost,
The bravest knight that we could boast.

So pass the chips, let's not be shy,
The clock just struck, oh my, oh my!
With stale old jokes and laughter bright,
We'll keep the fire burning all night.

Wrapped in a Blanket of Stars

Under the night, we gaze in awe,
At bright sparkles, we can't ignore.
A blanket spread, we snuggle tight,
While counting stars with all our might.

I swear I saw a shooting star,
But turned out it was just my car.
The constellations play disguise,
A pizza shape and fries—oh my!

With hot cocoa warming our hands,
We barter jokes and silly plans.
Like who can shout the loudest cheer,
That echoes back like "What's up, deer?"

Floating on dreams, while stars throw shade,
A cosmic dance that's fun, not fade.
Wrapped snug and warm, with smiles so bright,
In the canvas above, our hearts take flight.

Frost Kisses on Timeless Tales

Frosty windows, a chilly cheer,
As tales of winter draw us near.
Hot tea in hand, we laugh and tease,
About snowmen who refuse to freeze.

Grandma’s cookies, a frosty bake,
The secret’s salt? No, it’s a mistake!
Flour on noses and giggles galore,
As we munch through the snowy score.

Don’t forget the sledding tales told,
Where we soared high and felt so bold.
Only to tumble, all in a heap,
“Oh, where's my pants?” we laugh and weep!

So here’s to frost that makes us bright,
And stories that melt hearts, day or night.
In every flake, a memory spins,
Wrapped in laughter, warmth always wins.

Flickering Flames Against the Dark

Flames flicker, shadows dance,
In the evening's brief romance.
The ghost of dinner haunts the air,
Pasta gone wrong? A culinary scare!

We tell of blunders and slips so grand,
Like when the bread turned into sand.
With laughter rising like smoke above,
We toast to fails and our quest for love.

The dark may creep, but we won't cease,
Our tales bring warmth, a cozy fleece.
And when we snort at memories past,
It's clear that fun's forever cast.

So light the flame, let stories start,
For every laugh's a work of art.
With flickering flames and friendship tight,
We chase away the chilly night.

Memories as Thick as Snow

In winter's chill, we reminisce,
Snowball fights that we still miss.
Hot cocoa spilled on grandma's rug,
Laughter’s echo, a warm snug.

Frosty breaths like dragons' breath,
Sledding down hills, we flirted with death.
With mittens wet and cheeks aglow,
We vowed to build the world's best snow.

Lanterns Along the Path

Lanterns glowed like fireflies,
Guiding us through darkened skies.
We danced around, two left feet,
Tripping over branches, oh what a feat!

With every step, our shadows crept,
Where rabbits darted, we often leapt.
Then out popped a raccoon, oh dear!
We freaked and stumbled, ran in fear!

Beneath the Icy Veil

Underneath the ice so bright,
We dreamed of summers, warm delight.
Snowmen blink with buttons wide,
Trying to hide their frozen pride.

But in truth, they envy the sun,
While we throw snowballs, just for fun.
A snowplow roars, blocking our scene,
Winter's antics, always obscene!

Embraced by Snowflakes

Snowflakes danced down in a swirl,
Each one a unique little pearl.
Catching them on tongues was a treat,
Snowball battles, oh so sweet!

With pink noses and cheeks like a sprite,
We rolled in the snow till way past night.
Then home for hot soup, a glorious fate,
Eyes closed, dreaming of snowflakes great.

Kindred Spirits in Winter's Grip

Snowflakes fall, we start to slide,
Hot cocoa spills, let's take a ride.
Warm hats crooked, scarves unwound,
We'll laugh and trip on frozen ground.

Frosty breath, our giggles ring,
Penguins strut like an ice ballet fling.
Snowmen wobble with carrot noses,
Wishing they had warmer poses.

Winter games, a snowball fight,
Missed the mark, what a sight!
Chasing friends, we tumble down,
With frozen smiles, we wear the crown.

In winter's grip, we find our cheer,
Kindred spirits, never fear.
Through icy winds, our hearts stay bright,
Together we'll warm the coldest night.

Together in the Deep Blue Night

Under stars, we trip and fall,
Your coffee spills, you have a ball.
Moonlit laughs, our secrets shared,
Two big kids who never cared.

The sea's a-dark, waves crash and roar,
We dodge the splash, oh, what a chore!
The jellyfish dance, oh-so close,
Is that a fish? Or cheese on toast?

With sand in shoes, and salt on lips,
Our laughter brings the thundering ships.
Together we roam, in moonlight's glow,
Finding treasures, the tide's slow flow.

At midnight's door, our spirits soar,
In deep blue night, we seek for more.
With hearts aglow, we chase the light,
Forever friends, in wild delight.

A Tapestry of Warmth and Wonder

Knitting scarves, yarn takes flight,
Watch me tangle, what a sight!
Purls and stitches, welcome to my mess,
How did I make a net, no less?

Tea spills over, it's quite the show,
Laughter echoes, oh don't you know?
With each sip, we giggle and sigh,
Who needs a pattern? You and I!

Blanket forts where dreams take shape,
Adventures wild, no need for tape.
Together we weave sweet memories bright,
A tapestry built on pure delight.

So here's to warmth, in every way,
With love and wonder, come what may.
In our cozy nook, let's laugh and ponder,
Wrapped up tight, in joy and wonder.

Hearts Ignited in the Ice

Frozen lakes and skies of gray,
Yet here we dance, come what may.
With awkward moves, we slip and slide,
Grinning wide, no sense of pride.

Bonfire flames, we roast marshmallows,
S'mores gone rogue, stick to our bellows.
In every spark, our laughter flies,
Hearts ignited 'neath winter skies.

Chasing shadows in the night,
We're the silly from left to right.
Epic fails, but who would care?
In icy jaws, warmth is rare.

So let us bumble, laugh, and cheer,
In snowball battles, we’ve no fear.
With every slip, our spirits rise,
Hearts ignited, a sweet surprise.

The Chill of Magic Moments

In the chilly breeze, I saw a cat,
Wearing a hat, imagine that!
It winked at me, gave a sly grin,
Stealing my snack—where to begin?

We jumped on ice, slid with grace,
But lost our lunch—it fell from space!
Chasing snowflakes, we sneezed and rolled,
Who knew winter could be so bold?

Froze a tongue on a lollipop,
Only to trip and go splat! Ker-chop!
Magic moments, so funny and bright,
Even the snowballs laughed at our plight!

We made snowmen, a jolly lot,
But one turned into a giant pot!
Filled with soup that we tried to eat,
Left us shivering, can't be beat!

Embers in the Chill

At the campfire, under starlit skies,
S'mores went flying, oh what a surprise!
The marshmallows caught in a wild, fierce dance,
Sat on my shoe! Just my luck and chance!

Friend tried to roast a potato crisp,
But it launched like a rocket—what a wisp!
We laughed so hard, nearly fell in,
The chill of night disappeared with our grin!

We exchanged ghost stories, all rather lame,
'Til one popped up with a secret name!
To scare the socks off the bravest of men,
But all we got were hiccups again!

Embers glowed bright, a warm orange hue,
Like our belly laughs, our spirits grew.
In the chill, we found our funny flair,
Who needs a heater? There's laughter in the air!

Beneath the Silver Moon

Beneath the silver moon, oh what a sight,
I tripped on my shoelace, what a delight!
Caught my fall with a spin and a roll,
Now I’m a star in the moonlight stroll!

A cow jumped over to witness this show,
Mooing with laughter, putting on a glow.
The crickets giggled, the owls went, 'Whoo?'
As I redefined grace in front of the crew!

I danced with shadows, oh what a mess,
Two left feet in my fancy dress!
The moon glimmered down, with a cheeky flair,
As I tangled my hair in the cool night air.

But that night was magic, so funny and loud,
With laughter so bright, we felt quite proud.
Beneath the silver moon, we found our tune,
Making memories that’ll last till noon!

Flickering Memories

In the attic, dust bunnies play,
A photo of grandma, in her ballet.
“Do you remember?” I loudly ponder,
She said, “Of course, dear! Now where’s my thunder?”

Time travel’s tricky, I must confess,
My younger self wore far less stress.
I wore my cereal like a crown,
Now it's just a soggy brown frown.

Old toys in boxes, a treasure hoard,
A broken robot that just stored.
Memories flicker, like old TV,
Changing channels on life's comedy.

So let’s enjoy these giggling sights,
As we reminisce on those silly nights.
For if we forget, what’s left to find?
A dusty attic, a bewildered mind.

Cloaked in Softness

A pillow fort made with great finesse,
Cloaked in softness, it’s a true success.
Pillow fights erupt with squeals of delight,
Until the dog joins, what a fluffy fright!

Blankets piled, a mountain so grand,
We’ll take on the world, or at least the land.
With popcorn guns and fizzy soda streams,
We battle boredom with cozy dreams.

Cuddly bears provide wise advice,
“Life's more fun, with extra spice!”
In this fortress, we reign supreme,
Legends of softness, or so it seems.

But when mom calls, “Dinner!” we flee,
Leaving our kingdom for some broccoli.
We may be mighty in our soft domain,
But when it’s dinner, we’re all quite tame.

The Dance of Warmth and Cold

Winter blankets wrap the world in white,
While iced tea calls for summer's light.
The dance begins, a funny plight,
Do I wear shorts or cuddle up tight?

A snowman grins under golden rays,
While flip-flops prance in cold misty haze.
The thermostat as our referee,
Switching sides like a crazy spree.

Sipping cocoa, dodging the chill,
Then jumping in pools, what a thrill!
When hot meets cold in a twisty swirl,
You end up just like an ice cream whirl.

So we laugh and we groan, what fun is this?
Each season's a partner in the warmth and cold kiss.
Embrace the shift, let the calendar unfold,
A shimmering dance, forever bold.

Whispers on the Wind

The wind began to stir the leaves,
Whispers of secrets the branches weave.
“Did you hear that?” a squirrel did squeak,
“Someone forgot their socks. How bleak!”

Gossip flows through a feathered choir,
As tummies rumble by the campfire.
“Do they know it’s lunch?” the pine trees tease,
“Catch the wind, not the cold breeze!”

Clouds gossip freely, drifting high,
“I saw that storm, oh my, oh my!”
The sun just chuckles, a radiant grin,
“Let them have their fun, I’ll just spin!”

So listen closely to the airy sound,
Nature's comedies are all around.
In the rustling trees and whispers of skies,
A humorous tale in every sigh.

Nighttime's Gentle Embrace

The moon's a big cheese up high,
While stars are the mice that scurry by.
I tripped on my cat, oh what a sight,
He glared at me, 'This is my night!'

Bats hang upside down in glee,
Whispering secrets, just for me.
I wave to owls, they hoot back loud,
Living the dream, oh, ain't it proud?

The wind tells tales of ghosts that dance,
But really, it's just my pants' romance.
They wiggle and jiggle with every breeze,
Who knew my clothes had such expertise?

So here's to the night, with all its charms,
Blankets and pillows, oh they are arms.
Snuggling close in a sleepy embrace,
Then off to dreamland, at my own pace.

In the Hearth’s Soft Light

The fire crackles with a little pop,
My marshmallow flew, it took a flop.
S'mores on the floor, oh what a waste,
The dog looked at me with a hungry haste.

Grandpa's stories, they never quite land,
Of dragons and adventures, oh so grand.
But wait, what's that? A tale of woe?
The time the cat stole his sock from the blow!

Chairs creak like old bones with a groan,
As cousins argue, who’s on the phone?
A game of charades—who can guess right?
I mimed a giraffe, but just looked contrite.

In the hearth’s glow, with laughter we bask,
Sharing old jokes, it’s a big happy task.
With warmth in our hearts and snacks gone from sight,
We treasure the moments, all through the night.

Chasing Shadows in the Snow

Snowflakes fall like soft marshmallows,
I trudge through drifts, watch out for the shallows.
Footprints sprawl in a zig-zag dance,
But wait—what's that? A snowman in pants?

My gloves are soggy, my nose turns red,
Yet I can't help giggling at what I said.
"Snowball fight!" screams a cousin with flair,
I duck just in time—he's got quite the hair!

The sun dips low, shadows stretch tall,
Making a snow angel, I suddenly fall.
I lay there laughing, a fluffy white bed,
Who knew winter could mess with your head?

With cheeks like cherries, we head inside,
Hot cocoa awaits, it's sweet joy and pride.
Chasing shadows, in the snow, we play,
Memories made, come what may.

Laughter Beneath a Frosted Sky

The sky is frosted, oh what a sight,
We bundled up, all snug and tight.
But with each step, I trip and slide,
Like a baby deer, on winter's glide.

Laughter erupts as we tumble down,
Rolling like snowballs right in town.
"Who needs a sled?" I yell out loud,
We laugh so hard, we draw a crowd.

A dog joins in, with a bark and a spin,
Chasing his tail, oh where's the win?
He leaps through the snow, so full of quilt,
Knocking me over—with snow he's built!

Under the frosted sky, we gleefully cheer,
For winter's wonders that bring us near.
With warmth in our hearts and snow on our toes,
We laugh and we play, as hot cocoa flows.

Hearthside Reveries

Sipping cocoa, my cat’s in a trance,
She dreams of fish, oh, the feline romance.
The fire crackles with stories untold,
While my socks are mismatched, both faded and old.

The kettle whistles a tune that I know,
Like a disco party for the marshmallow dough.
The flames dance wildly, a showtime delight,
Who knew staying home could be this out of sight?

My dog’s on the couch, all wrapped in a quilt,
Snoring so loudly, I'm starting to wilt.
I left him some pizza, fresh from last night,
Now he's plotting revenge—what a comical fright!

Outside, snowflakes are falling like loot,
While I'm in my PJs, donning my boot.
Bring on the winter, the frost, and the cheer,
With laughter and snacks, I shall have no fear!

Conversations Wrapped in Wool

Snug in my blanket, a yarn in my hand,
I ponder on life, and its weird little strands.
The sweater I knit looks more like a dish,
I'll call it abstract and hope that's my wish.

My friend on the couch is unraveling jokes,
A llama with glasses, now that's how it pokes.
We laugh till it hurts, with our tea in a spin,
Who knew knitting could lead to such giddy sins?

The dog tries to help, but he's tangled in thread,
A scarf for a mouse? That's what he just said.
We watch as each stitch forms a comical plot,
In a world full of fluff, who cares what we've wrought?

As winter's chill whispers through frosted panes,
We warm our hearts with ridiculous gains.
With laughter and warmth, wrapped together in wool,
These memories we weave, oh what a delightful fool!

Glimmers of Joy in Winter's Night

The moon is a pie, just baked for tonight,
While snowflakes are giggling, oh what a sight.
The squirrel looks puzzled, wearing a hat,
As he steals all my nuts—what a chittering brat!

Icicles shimmer like diamonds on trees,
While my nose is red like a dog’s favorite tease.
I tripped on the sidewalk, a slapstick ballet,
Perhaps winter sports are just not my forte.

The stars are confetti in a dark velvet sky,
And I stand here dreaming of clouds drifting by.
With cocoa and goodies, I'm ready to cheer,
Join me for laughs, let’s spread warmth, my dear!

So gather around, let’s dance in delight,
For winter and laughter can make our hearts light.
With joy like a snowman, we'll wiggle and sway,
These glimmers of joy will forever hold sway!

The Bond Beyond the Breeze

Two penguins tango, with tuxedos on tight,
They waddle and twirl in a frosty moonlight.
With icy cool moves and a shimmy so fine,
They thrill all the seals—oh, they're one of a kind!

The wind whispers secrets to trees standing tall,
While the snowmen rejoice in their winter ball.
They swap silly hats and engage in strange games,
'Tis a ruckus of giggles, all bursting with flames!

The owls are wise, but their puns are quite lame,
Who knew their hoots would bring so much fame?
With a wink and a nod, they join in the tease,
And laughter takes flight on the cold winter's breeze.

So here we stand, laughing under the stars,
With friends made of snow, and hot chocolate jars.
This bond that we share, warmth wrapped in the freeze,
Is a treasure that dances in life's winter breeze!

A Tapestry of Warmth

In winter's clutch, we wear our best,
A quilt of layers, we're all dressed.
Hats that won't fit, gloves missing pairs,
We look like marshmallows, but who cares!

The heater roars, a cheerful friend,
With baked potato vibes until the end.
Sipping soup like royalty on a throne,
Who needs summer when warmth's overblown!

The couch is a ship, we drift and sway,
Remote in hand, we'll binge all day.
Why step outside into the cold?
When right here, a cozy tale unfolds!

So let it snow, let the wind blow wild,
We'll wrap ourselves up, like a happy child.
In this tapestry of warmth so bright,
We find our joy on a winter's night.

The Comfort of Snowfall

Snowflakes tumble, a frosty dance,
On everyone's hats, they take their chance.
A snowball fight? Oh, what a sight!
But watch your back, it's all in good fright!

Sledding down hills with giggles and cheer,
While frozen fingers shed not a tear.
Hot cocoa waits with marshmallows afloat,
A sip of happiness in a cozy coat!

Frosty breath in the chilly air,
All bundled up, we are quite the pair.
But slip on ice, and what's that noise?
Oops! Down we go, oh how it enjoys!

The world is white and the cheer is grand,
With snowmen built like a vibrant band.
So grab your mittens, let's make some more,
The comfort of snowfall brings us to explore!

Luminous Dreams in January

January dawns with a dazzling glow,
We promise ourselves, 'This year we'll glow.'
But breakfast calls with snooze in our eyes,
Luminous dreams become cloudy sighs.

New Year's resolutions? Oh, what a joke!
I'll read more books, eat less cake—oh poke!
Yet here I am, with pie on my face,
Plans crumble fast in this wintry race.

The treadmill stares, it beckons my name,
But Netflix whispers, 'Come join the game!'
Yoga mat rolled, it gathers some dust,
While I binge-watch dramas—oh, how I lust!

So here's to January, chilly and bright,
With dreams that twinkle like stars in the night.
Next year I'll try—as I do every fall,
But for now, let's just enjoy it all!

Jackets and Jubilation

Out come the jackets, zippers galore,
Layer upon layer—who could want more?
Scarves wrapped tightly, we resemble a mummy,
But at least we’re warm and feeling quite chummy!

Boots that squeak with each joyful step,
Walking like penguins, we barely adept.
Jumping in puddles, who knew it’s fun?
A splash of a snowdrift—that’s how we run!

In parks, we gather, our laughter rings clear,
With snowmen towering, it's festive cheer.
Hot cider serves warmth, like a hug in a cup,
Jackets and jubilation, we’ll never give up!

So winter, embrace us with all your chill,
With frosted breath and joyous thrill.
For in every jacket, there’s a heart that beats,
In jubilation, our happiness repeats!

Cherished in the Cold

Winter's here and I am froze,
Hugging my cocoa like a rose.
The snowflakes dance like tiny spies,
While I wear socks that look like pies.

The wind it howls, a ghostly tune,
My only friend's a plastic spoon.
It stirs my dreams of sugar lanes,
While I sip on soup and dodge the pains.

I've got a scarf that's way too long,
It trips me up like a silly song.
But wrapped in warmth, I can't complain,
And make a throne from pillows' reigns.

So here I sit, a cozy brat,
With fashionable sweatpants, fancy that!
In winter's chill, I find my glee,
Embraced by blankets, just me and me.

Huddled in Tenderness

My cat and I are quite the pair,
She takes my snacks, I take her hair.
Side by side in a bundle tight,
We share our warmth each chilly night.

Each paw that lands is quite absurd,
She stretches, yawns, and gives a word.
I talk to her, she stares with glee,
"More treats!" she purrs, "Come cuddle me!"

The couch becomes our little throne,
Where every whisper feels like home.
In this huddle, life feels sound,
With laughter echoing all around.

So here we nest, no thought of time,
With her big eyes and my silly rhyme.
In this warm nook, we've found our bliss,
With a cozy hug and a furry kiss.

Breaths of Silver

With every breath, I puff out air,
I whistle tunes, pretend to care.
The mirror laughs, it sees me grinning,
As I inhale, my day's beginning.

Oh, to be crisp, like frosty dew,
But all I get is a sneeze or two.
I dance with clouds that swirl and churn,
While snacking on the softest fern.

My friends all say, "You've got some flair!"
I giggle softly, "It's the air!"
In this breath game, I'm leading well,
Inhaling joy, exhaling a spell.

So here's to lungs, so bright and spry,
With every puff, I touch the sky.
I'll take a chance, breathe deep and boldly,
In the mist of life, I am so moldy!

The Inner Hearth

Deep in my heart, there's a little flame,
It cracks and pops, but I feel no shame.
An inner hearth, where my hopes are grilled,
Serving up dreams that keep me thrilled.

With logs of laughter and kindling cheer,
I toast my marshmallows, sipping beer.
The embers glow, they whisper bright,
Keeping me warm on this chilly night.

I throw in worries like kindling twigs,
Watch them fizzle and dance like pigs.
"Be gone!" I shout, "You silly stress!"
As I feast on humor, full of zest.

So let it blaze and let it roar,
For my inner hearth will never bore.
With every spark, I'll sing my tune,
In the warmth of joy, I find my boon.

Firelight Fantasies

In the glow of flames so bright,
I thought I saw a dragon's flight.
Turns out it was my cat's wild chase,
With a marshmallow on its face!

The shadows leap, they twist and scream,
I ponder if this is a dream.
The fire's crackle starts to sing,
About a knight who lost his ring!

The logs they snap, they dance and sway,
I join the flames in this ballet.
But singed eyebrows tell me clear,
Perhaps I've danced a bit too near!

So here I laugh, I smile, I jest,
With firelight that's truly the best.
I'll toast some s'mores to seal the fate,
Of a night that won't hesitate!

Hearth-stitched Love

In the cozy nook, we both reside,
With my blanket on, you're warm inside.
But when you steal the last of fries,
I can't help but roll my eyes!

Your socks are mismatched, I must confess,
Yet your laugh, it leaves me in a mess.
With pizza crumbs all in your beard,
You still claim I'm the one revered!

We binge-watch shows till we get sore,
Every season just leaves us wanting more.
But when you sprawl, taking my space,
I admit it brings a smile to my face!

In our little world of oddity,
Each day is filled with comedy.
So let's sip tea and flip some toast,
For our hearth-stitched love, I gladly boast!

Glittering Nights

Stars above are shining bright,
But so is my neighbor's porch light.
With twinkling lights that look so fine,
I dread to ask, 'Is that all mine?'

The moon is full, it starts to glow,
Yet my glow sticks steal the show.
With silly dancing suits in sight,
Who needs a club when it's this night?

My friends and I form a dancing chain,
Tripping over each other's pain.
A slip, a fall, we laugh and squeal,
Is there a night that feels more real?

We set our dreams in quirky flight,
In glittering chaos, pure delight.
So let's toast to this magical place,
And hope tomorrow's just as ace!

Cherished Days

From sunny morns to laughing nights,
Each moment feels like soaring kites.
Yet socks that vanish, oh what a crime,
They choose to hide, they have no time!

Coffee spills and pancake fights,
We mix up wrongs and do it right.
Recipes fail but still we try,
A chef's delight turns to a pie!

Puzzles we share, pieces gone mad,
“Where’s the corner?” makes us sad.
But through the chaos, joy appears,
With cherished days full of silly cheers!

Life’s little quirks bring us near,
In laughter, we find love sincere.
So here's a toast to our funny ways,
Let’s make memories in cherished days!

Flames dancing with Frost

In winter’s chill, while fires burn bright,
The frost outside gives such a fright.
But here we roast, the marshmallows sing,
As chilly winds around us swing.

A turtleneck and a woolly hat,
I cuddle up, and there's the cat.
He steals my heat, oh woe is me,
But he’s too cute, I let it be!

From flames that crackle, we hear them moan,
They say “stay close”, don’t be alone.
Yet frosty noses touch the heat,
A duet that can’t be beat!

So here we are, through hot and cold,
With tales of warmth that must be told.
In this odd dance of frost and flame,
We find the joy that feels the same!

A Toast to the Cold

Grab your mittens and your hat,
Raise your glass and have a chat.
Snowflakes fall like little shouts,
Winter’s here, let’s warm our snouts.

Hot cocoa flows, it’s quite the treat,
Sipping slow, let’s warm our feet.
Frosty noses, cheeks aglow,
To the freeze, we say, "Hello!"

Laughter echoes through the chill,
Snowball fights, a winter thrill.
Bring on flurries, we don’t mind,
With a drink, we’re feeling fine!

So here’s to snow and chilly nights,
To cozy socks and indoor fights.
Raise your glass, let’s sing aloud,
In winter’s chill, we’re all quite proud!

Dancing Shadows

In the moonlight, shadows prance,
Beneath the trees, they take a chance.
Twisting, turning, what a sight,
Are they dancing? Oh, delight!

Goblins grin and fairies spin,
Join the fun; let laughter win.
Just beware of the broomstick sweep,
Or into the shadows you might leap!

They jig around the flickering flame,
Each one claiming a funny name.
Hop along, and don't be shy,
In shadows we will surely fly!

So grab your partner, step in time,
Add some giggles, make it rhyme.
In the night, we laugh and shout,
With dancing shadows, there's no doubt!

Hope in the Dark

When night falls and worries creep,
Remember hope is yours to keep.
A glow appears, so soft, so bright,
Chasing shadows out of sight.

Light a candle, share a smile,
Stay with me, it's worth the while.
Even in darkness, we can gleam,
Hold my hand, let's dare to dream.

With laughter ringing, hearts will soar,
Hope is knocking at the door.
In midnight's hush, dreams take flight,
Let's find that spark, ignite the night!

So when the clouds begin to roam,
Remember, you are never alone.
With friends and giggles, joy's embarked,
Hand in hand, we'll light the dark!

Winter's Caress

The snowflakes kiss our noses cold,
Winter’s touch is pure and bold.
Wrap your scarf and stomp your feet,
Let’s embrace this frosty treat!

Icicles dangle, shimmering bright,
Nature’s jewels in the moonlight.
With each flake, a giggle shared,
In winter’s arms, we’re unprepared!

Snowmen grinning near the door,
Giant snowballs on the floor.
Hot cider waiting on the stove,
Winter’s magic, we all love!

So grab your sled, let’s race outside,
With happy hearts, we’ll take the ride.
To winter’s caress, let’s shout hooray,
In frosty fun, we’ll play all day!

A Sanctuary of Warmth in the Cold

In winter's chill, we gather 'round,
With mugs of cocoa, joy is found.
We share our tales, both silly and bold,
In this warm haven, let the laughter unfold.

The fireplace crackles, telling its jokes,
As we roast marshmallows and poke fun at folks.
A blanket fort built with eyes all aglow,
In this sanctuary, our worries can't flow.

The snowflakes dance outside our door,
While we spill secrets and giggle for more.
With hats and mittens all piled high,
In this cozy retreat, our spirits will fly.

So here's to this warmth, to friendship's bright fate,
We'll cherish this laughter, it's never too late.
With love and humor wrapped snug as a burrito,
In winter's embrace, we're a giggly bunch of amigos.

The Radiance of Friendship's Glow

Like candles flickering in the night,
Friendship shines, oh what a sight!
We gather round, sharing our dreams,
In this warm glow, nothing is as it seems.

We swap our snacks with giggles and grace,
Each bite brings a smile to every face.
From cookies to chips, we munch and chat,
Friendship's feast, now that's where it's at!

We paint the world in colors so bright,
With inside jokes that take flight.
Our laughter echoes like a joyous tune,
In this golden glow under the moon.

As the stars twinkle in the wide dark sky,
We toast to the moments that zip by.
With hearts so warm and spirits so high,
Our friendship's light will never say goodbye.

Cozy Corners of Shared Dreams

In cozy corners, we plot and plan,
With visions of grandeur, and maybe a tan.
We mix up our dreams like kids in a jar,
With hopes that stretch near and far.

Our laughter spills like confetti rain,
Drowning our worries, easing the pain.
We scribble ideas on napkins and walls,
In cozy corners, we conquer it all.

With snacks in hand and a spark in our eyes,
We craft our futures, just one little surprise.
From silly schemes to wild dreams of gold,
In every corner, adventures unfold.

So here’s to the dreamers in chairs that recline,
Crafting great stories over glasses of wine.
In cozy corners, our spirits will soar,
Sharing our dreams, who could ask for more?

Melodies of Laughter and Snowflakes

As snowflakes fall like soft little dancers,
We break out the snacks and take some chances.
With snowballs flying in a joyful brawl,
Laughter echoes, cradling us all.

Hot chocolate rivers splash on our clothes,
Each sip a reminder of how friendship grows.
With whipped cream mountains piled so high,
In this snowy wonder, we jump and fly.

We sing silly songs; off-key is the game,
Yet our voices rise just the same.
In this flurry of fun, we all take a bow,
Melodies of laughter, here and now.

With snowflakes swirling, our hearts feel light,
Friendship's warmth against the cold bite.
So let's make some noise, let's dance in the snow,
For the best memories come from laughter's glow.

Fireside Chatters

The flames dance and flicker bright,
S'mores fly like birds in flight.
Granny's tales of ghosts at night,
Make us giggle till it’s light.

The marshmallows roast to a perfect tan,
But the chocolate won’t stick to the pan.
Then Uncle Joe cracks a silly pun,
And we all laugh till we're done.

Our socks are warm, the stories bold,
As snoring grandpa breaks the mold.
A nighttime symphony unfolds,
With fireside chatters we behold.

So gather 'round, don’t be a bore,
For laughter's worth more than s'mores!
We're wrapped in joy, from nose to toes,
In our hearts, the warmth still glows.

Hearts of Gold in Chilly Skies

In winter's chill, we strut with pride,
With hats too big and scarves that slide.
Our hearts of gold, they cannot hide,
Amidst the snowflakes, we take a ride.

The snowmen grumble, their noses askew,
With carrots stolen by the puppy crew.
We laugh at their plight, oh what to do,
In this winter wonderland so askew!

Hot cocoa spills, a chocolate flood,
We slip and slide in a snowy mud.
But friendships warm like a fireplace bud,
In chilly skies we're never a dud.

With sleds that crash and laughter loud,
We celebrate winter, joyous and proud.
Together we stand, icy and cowed,
In hearts of gold, we’re wrapped in a shroud.

Touched by Hearthlight

In the glow of the fire's embrace,
Socks and slippers, a cozy space.
Grandpa's tales, a silly race,
With pie on his shirt, all over the place.

The cat snores loud, dreaming of fish,
As Aunt Sue whips up a bizarre dish.
It’s the kind of meal that makes us wish
For takeout instead, but we savor it swish.

We recount the days with feathers and glue,
Of sledding trips gone askew.
Our hearts are full, our spirits renew,
As warm as a hug, and twice as true.

So let’s gather near, with laughter in sight,
For we are all touched by hearthlight.
In every chuckle and quirky delight,
We create a bond that feels just right.

The Winter of Our Stories

As snowflakes tumble, stories ignite,
From snowball fights to hot cocoa nights.
We gather 'round, with warmth in sight,
In the winter's grip, our hearts take flight.

With every tale of clumsiness shared,
We reminisce of times we dared.
From slippery falls to being impaired,
In this icy wonderland, we're all prepared.

Uncle Dave juggles and drops the pies,
The laughter erupts, the joy never dies.
In the winter of stories, mischief flies,
Our memories sparkle like starlit skies.

So let's write more tales, let laughter flow,
In this snowy season where friendships grow.
With each whispered joke, our hearts aglow,
In the winter of our stories, let's steal the show.

Candles Against the Ice

In winter's grip, the candles gleam,
They dance and flicker, like a dream.
Yet one took flight, oh what a sight,
A puppy tried to catch it, what a fright!

With flames that wave and shadows lurk,
My cat just stares; he’s gone berserk.
He thinks he’s brave, a little chump,
But runs away with a single thump!

We gather 'round, with mugs in hand,
Recalling tales, so bold and grand.
But as I laugh, a candle's wax,
Drips right on me—oh, how it attacks!

Now warmth is here, but with a twist,
The ice still laughs; I can't resist.
For winter nights, with all their spice,
Are best enjoyed with candles—ice!

Fireside Reverie

By the fire, we share our dreams,
Of summer sun and ice cream screams.
A marshmallow's fate, stuck on a stick,
Caught in a flame, that made me quick!

The dog's on guard, his tail a-blur,
Thinking of all, he'll strongly stir.
But give him a snack, and just like that,
He's gone to snooze—where's my chitchat?

The stories flow like melted snow,
As sparks of laughter start to glow.
But when I trip, it's onward I fly,
Right into the lap of my dear pie guy!

With giggles and warmth, we close our eyes,
Imagining summer, beneath clear skies.
But winter's still here, frosty and sly,
So let's put on marshmallows and ask "Why?"

The Glow of Winter's Embrace

As winter rolls in with icy breath,
We gather ‘round to cheat the death.
With cocoa cups and cookies near,
The only real worry: what's that deer?

They come for crumbs, oh what a tease,
While we huddle tight, with utmost ease.
But when one sneezes, off they dash,
Leaving us laughing, with quite the splash!

The glow of lights sets hearts ablaze,
But my neighbor’s tunes leave me in a daze.
They sing carols loud, out of key,
I swear I heard a cat’s plea!

So here we sit, in this quirky space,
Finding our laughter, a warm embrace.
With winter outside, cold and bright,
I’ll keep sharing cookies 'til morning light!

Cuddle Under the Stars

Let's snuggle tight beneath the sky,
Where stars twinkle like they're shy.
The blanket slips, and oh what fun,
A race for warmth, we nearly run!

The chilly breeze just loves to tease,
While we sip tea, as if it's free.
But all it takes is one small sneeze,
And all our blankets fly like leaves!

The moon beams down, with a smile wide,
It knows of our frolics, we cannot hide.
So here we are, in our tangle of laughter,
For warmth and joy is what we're after!

As we gaze up, hear this refrain,
Winter will come, but it's not in vain.
For love and joy under stars that twinkle,
Is the kind of warmth that makes hearts crinkle!

Heartbeats Beneath a White Canopy

Roses in snow, how absurd,
A snowman that just won't get stirred.
Fingers get cold, but lips stay warm,
Love in winter is a unique charm.

Sledding down hills, I take a tumble,
My partner laughs, oh how I stumble!
Hot cocoa spills all over my face,
But laughter's the warmth we both embrace.

Giant boots sticking in the air,
Trying to dance, but who’s aware?
Snowflakes landing on my nose,
Cupid’s arrows, that’s how it goes!

Under this blanket, soft and white,
We scheme to sneak chocolate, what a delight!
Heartbeats thumping, snowflakes twirl,
In winter's chill, love gives a whirl.

S’mores Under the Ice

Building a fire, but all I see,
Is frozen marshmallows staring at me.
Graham crackers melted, what a sight,
It’s like they lost a heat-fighting fight!

Chocolate bar's stuck to my glove,
Wishing instead I had a stove.
Fire’s an icicle, what a tease,
Should've known better than to freeze!

Lights twinkle, I’m dreaming of goo,
Instead I've got frost, and that’s not cool.
But who needs sweets? I’ll take a laugh,
As we nibble on chips, what a silly craft!

Under the stars, our giggles sprout,
S’mores made of frost? I doubt!
Yet here we are with laughter in tow,
Love's warmth outshines this icy show.

Winter's Embrace

Wrapped in layers, I can hardly wiggle,
Caught in the snow, what a chilly giggle.
Snowflakes tangle in my hair,
Winter fashion? A snowman affair.

We trudge through drifts for a holiday feast,
Where's the turkey? Is it chilled or released?
Frosty beverage in hand, I cheer,
That’s just frozen soda – oh dear!

Snowball fights become an art,
With chilly ammo, I’m quick to start.
Laughter erupts as I make my aim,
But it’s me getting hit, what a shame!

Night falls softly, stars do ignite,
Winter's embrace, a warming delight.
In this frosty air, I find my grace,
With you beside me, time we cannot chase.

The Flames of Affection

A campfire crackles, sparks to the sky,
Forgot marshmallows? Oh my, oh my!
Flames dancing, shadows ducking around,
Wait, is that smoke? Or love I have found?

With my love near, I feel so warm,
Even when embers start to swarm.
You tell a joke, I can't help but snort,
Laughter ignites, of the best sort!

Hearts racing fast, like a match to a wick,
We sip our cider, it's quite the trick.
But when you steal fries from my plate,
I declare war – this love can't wait!

So here we toast to our silly fate,
With silly giggles, we can't hesitate.
Though our culinary skills might lack,
In the flames of affection, we'll never look back.

Embers in the Chill

The fire's dim, the sparks do dance,
A marshmallow fell, gone in a glance.
Snowflakes dive from the sky so gray,
Is it winter or are we just at play?

Scents of pine, and cocoa too,
A holiday sweater, bright and blue.
The dog stole the blanket, what a fuss!
Now I'm chilly, but not as much as Gus!

A snowman winks with a carrot nose,
He's been here longer than any of those!
Chasing squirrels as he starts to melt,
Funny how that snowman really dealt!

Embers fade but laughter stays,
Telling tales of our winter ways.
The chill outside can bring a cheer,
With funny friends, winter's held dear.

Hearthside Whispers

By the hearth, the tales unfold,
Of furry beasts and treasures bold.
A cat named Mittens, proud and sly,
Claims the warm spot with a little sigh.

Hot chocolate spills, what a sight!
The mugs are dancing, what a fright!
The puppy’s chewing on grandma's shoe,
It seems he thinks it's a toy too!

Tickling toes in fuzzy socks,
As winter winds rattles the clocks.
We giggle loud, we howl with glee,
What’s a winter without some pee?

So let’s huddle and share a grin,
These hearthside whispers among kin.
Snowflakes land atop our heads,
While warm inside, so are our beds.

Beneath a Frosted Moon

The moon shines bright, a frosted gem,
As squirrels plan their midnight mayhem.
Beneath the stars, the silence sings,
With fluffy blankets and silly things.

A snowball fight, oh what a blast!
We threw and we laughed, until we gasped.
A tumble here, a slip or two,
Winter’s laughter is always true.

Hot cider waits as we rush back in,
Frosted cheeks with a silly grin.
Imagine if the moon could talk,
He'd laugh with us, with every shock!

So raise your cups and toast the night,
Under frosted moons, our spirits ignite.
With friends by your side, don't be a zombie,
Embrace the fun, like it’s our hobby!

Snuggled in the Cold

Wrapped in blankets, a cozy sight,
With popcorn bowls and movies light.
The thermostat’s on its final breath,
Yet we chuckle, defying death!

A penguin waddles across the screen,
Does he know he's part of the gleam?
With big eyes wide, we can't believe,
That winter's chill, we can retrieve!

A chicken dance in socks is bold,
As we heat up, despite the cold.
Laughing loud at our frozen fate,
Winter's chill can’t seal our fate!

So here's to us, in our warm embrace,
Finding joy in this snowy space.
Snuggled in the warmth so tight,
Turns out winter's a sheer delight!

Hot Chocolate Dreams

In a cup of cocoa, so warm and neat,
Marshmallows dance, a sugary treat.
Whipped cream clouds float high above,
Sipping this joy, I'm in love.

Chocolate rivers, oh what a sight,
I'll drink them all, day and night.
With sprinkles that giggle and swirl so fast,
In this dreamland, I’m hoping it’ll last.

A cocoa mustache, oh what a look,
It’s my favorite chapter from the cookbook.
Laughter bubbles like frothy foam,
In this chocolate bliss, I've found my home.

So bring on the mugs, let's have a cheer,
For hot chocolate dreams, let's all draw near!
With laughter and joy, let’s raise our cup,
To our marshmallow dreams, oh fill it up!

Saffron Sunsets

The sun dips low, an orange glow,
Saffron skies put on a show.
Clouds drifting by with a cotton candy hue,
As day waves goodbye, what a view!

Birds tuning up for a nighttime song,
Chirping sweetly, they can't go wrong.
A blanket of stars, so shiny and bright,
Dancing like fireflies in the night.

But wait, what's that in the fading light?
A squirrel wearing shades, what a sight!
He squawks and he hops, full of flair,
Even the trees can’t help but stare.

So let’s laugh at the sunset's grace,
As the saffron sky paints our face.
With giggles and gleams, let's enjoy the ride,
Under saffron sunsets, where dreams abide!

Snowflakes and Serenades

Snowflakes twirl like ballerinas so bold,
Dancing in the winter, a sight to behold.
Each one unique, a frosty design,
Just like my socks, mismatched but fine.

A serenade sung by a friendly owl,
He hoots on the branch with an elegant scowl.
“Whoo's there?” he asks with a wink and a nod,
As snowflakes giggle, giving him a prod.

Children in scarves make snowmen so round,
With carrots for noses they’re quite profound.
A snowball fight breaks out in a wee,
Covered in snow, I shout with glee!

So let’s twirl and sway in this flurry of fun,
With snowflakes and serenades, we’ve only begun.
We’ll dance through the night ‘neath the winter's embrace,

In a world filled with laughter, let’s find our place!

Whispered Secrets in the Dark

In the dark, shadows play,
Whispered secrets come out to sway.
A giggle escapes from a closet tight,
Did the cat just say, “Let’s party tonight?”

Moonlight spills through the window neat,
Illuminating socks lost on my feet.
Monsters in blankets, so fluffy and sweet,
Join in the fun, don’t skip a beat.

A murmur of dreams, discussing the stars,
Who thinks aliens drive goofy cars?
Under the covers, we snicker and grin,
Making our plans for a whirlwind spin.

When dawn arrives, these secrets will fade,
However, in memories, they won’t evade.
Whispered friendships in the dark, a spark,
Let's cherish the laughter, let’s leave our mark!

Milton Keynes UK
Ingram Content Group UK Ltd.
UKHW021403081224
452111UK00007B/127

9 789916 909560